HENRI NOUWEN

Illuminated

HENRI NOUWEN
Illuminated

Len Sroka

ACTA
PUBLICATIONS

Henri Nouwen Illuminated
by Len Sroka

Edited by Gregory F. Augustine Pierce
Artwork by www.seescapes.com
Typesetting by Desktop Edit Shop, Inc.
Design consultation by Larry Taylor Design, Ltd.

Quotations by Henri J.M. Nouwen accompanying the images are from the book cited beneath the lower right corner of each image. Sources and permissions are listed in the credits on the final page of the book. Thanks to the publishers and to the Henri Nouwen Society (www.henrinouwen.org) for their encouragement.

Published by ACTA Publications, Assisting Christians To Act, 5559 W. Howard Street, Skokie, IL 60077-2621, 800-397-2282, www.actapublications.com

Library of Congress Catalog number: 2005924404
ISBN: 0-87946-288-4
Printed in the Republic of Korea
Year 10 09 08 07 06 05
Printing 10 9 8 7 6 5 4 3 2 1

Contents

Dedication

To Henri Nouwen, whom I've long considered my spiritual "older brother." His courageous and heartfelt sharing of his spiritual life continues to help me live mine.

Introduction

Each of Henri Nouwen's books invites us to open our eyes to God's presence in the nooks and crannies of our souls and our world. In the final years of his life, Nouwen – priest, professor and writer – found a physical and spiritual home among the handicapped residents of L'Arche Daybreak Community, whom he found to be his most powerful spiritual advisors.

Nouwen's words invite us to join his quest for living a spiritual life in the nitty-gritty of our daily lives, in the here-and-now. This book considers his spiritual direction from the perspective of three fundamental invitations:

- Develop a Spiritual Perspective – increase awareness of the spiritual dimension of our lives
- Nurture Our Spiritual Nature – encourage the growth of the contemplative dimension of our lives
- Share Our Spiritual Life – share the fruits of our awareness with our sisters and brothers

The photo-meditations in this book strive to provide a setting for the depth of Nouwen's words. In the ancient tradition of "illuminated manuscripts" the power of his words are augmented by the power of the images.

For more than twenty years the words of Henri Nouwen have nourished my life. As I've read and reread his works over the years, I've underlined and highlighted core bits of wisdom that seemed to pop out of the page at me.

Over the last ten years, I've been merging photographic images on my computer to help envision the words of visionaries like Nouwen. For me, building each photo-illustration layer after layer has become a contemplative experience by which I more deeply enter the spirit of the writings of my spiritual mentors. This book evolved from a series of photo-meditations I created to share the thoughts of these remarkable spiritual visionaries on my website ministry, www.seescapes.com.

I hope the photo-meditations in this book illuminate for you the wisdom of Henri Nouwen.

Section 1

Develop Your Spiritual Perspective

"Is there a God in this world?" Henri Nouwen believed that this is the central question of our spiritual life. To answer this question he challenges us to begin seeing ourselves for what we truly are – the beloved children of God. The first step in gaining a spiritual perspective on our lives is to "Dare to Be Loved."

Once we begin accepting ourselves as the beloved of God, we "Come Home" – we begin to live in the loving home that God has made in our hearts. We begin to see how many ways God is a living and active presence in all that we do.

But seeing ourselves as the beloved-of-God is a challenge. So often we feel unloved. We need to "Dare to Be Human" – to accept our mortal reality while claiming our soul-deep union with the divine.

This process of gradually gaining a spiritual perspective is a daily discipline in which we "Learn God's Ways." Every person we meet can offer us a glimpse of God. Every earthly thing can become a sacred window.

Chapter 1

Dare to Be Loved

One of the most difficult things for us to believe is that we are each a beloved child of God. How often do we recognize this? How often do we allow ourselves to live this core truth of our identity?

Nouwen reminds us time and again that God's one response to each of us is: "You are my Beloved, on you my favor rests." In a way we cannot fathom, each of us is God's favorite.

From all eternity God has seen each of us as "unique, special, precious beings." Accepting God's love, Nouwen feels, makes us better human beings, while enabling us to make our world a better place.

When our life becomes a burden, we need to remind ourselves again and again that we are loved with an everlasting love. Our Father embraces us with the heart and arms of a loving Mother.

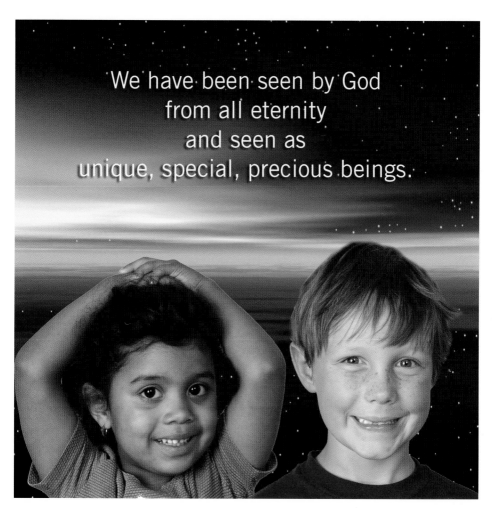

We have been seen by God
from all eternity
and seen as
unique, special, precious beings.

Life of the Beloved

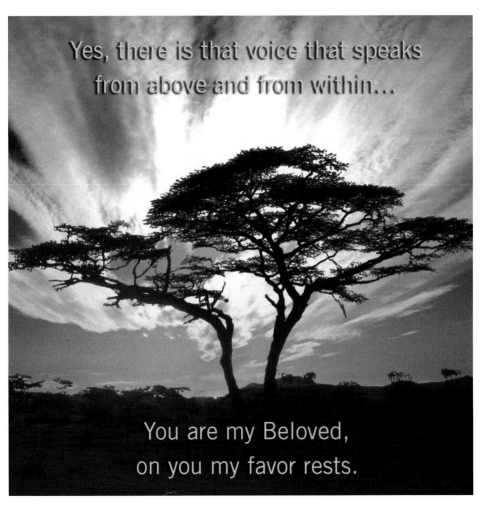

Yes, there is that voice that speaks from above and from within...

You are my Beloved, on you my favor rests.

Life of the Beloved

I cannot fathom how
all of God's children can be favorites.
And still, they are.

The Return of the Prodigal Son

God wants to come close, very close,
so close that we can rest
in the intimacy of God
as children in their mother's arms.

Finding My Way Home

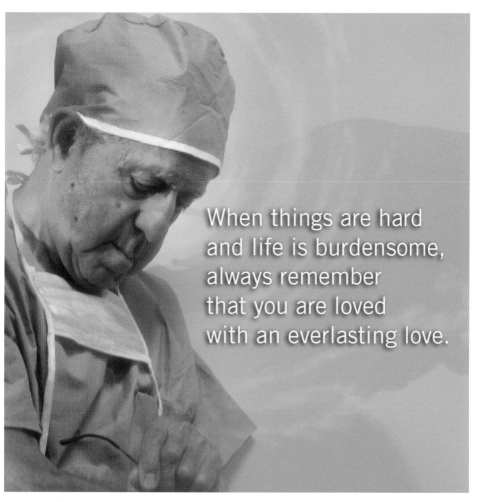

When things are hard
and life is burdensome,
always remember
that you are loved
with an everlasting love.

Life of the Beloved

Our life is a short opportunity
to say "yes" to God's love.

Here and Now

Chapter 2

Come Home

*O*ur whole life is an ongoing search for a place we can really call home. God knows how much we yearn for a home. Much of Nouwen's writings point to that inner space in each of us where God dwells and in which we are invited to live with God.

Living the spiritual life, as Nouwen sees it, is living in God's house here and now. Yet time and again our life drifts away. To come home we need to move away from places in which God is no longer with us. We need to come home, again and again.

God is always looking for us and will go anywhere to find us. God wants us home. Our hearts were created with a yearning that only the divine spirit can fill.

God so much desired to fulfill
our deepest yearning for a home
that God decided to build
a home in us.

Lifesigns

God is looking for you.
He will go anywhere to find you.
He loves you, he wants you home.

The Return of the Prodigal Son

Move away from the places
where God is no longer with you.

The Inner Voice of Love

Through the spiritual life
we gradually move
from the house of fear
to the house of love.

Behold the Beauty of the Lord

There is a space within us
where God dwells
and where we are invited
to dwell with God.

Here and Now

God created in our heart
a yearning for communion
that no one but God can,
and wants, to fulfill.

With Burning Hearts

Chapter 3

Dare to Be Human

We're only human. We are wounded physically, emotionally, mentally, spiritually. But that's all right, Nouwen assures us. Even in our flawed and frightened condition we are the beloved children of God.

We are divided people – divided against ourselves, each other, and God. We are doubters, but we have it in us to be believers. The spiritual life helps us bridge the gap between who we now are and who we are called to become.

We who dare to hope live in the trust that our life is in good hands. We are ready to be surprised by the grace that can burst forth from the depth of our pain. We're only human, but God wants to share divinity with us.

Our life is...a time in which sadness and joy kiss each other at every moment.

Out of Solitude

All of us are
'two people'
a doubting one and a believing one.

The Genesee Diary

I am praying while not knowing how to pray,
I am resting while feeling restless,
at peace while tempted,
safe while still anxious...

The Road to Daybreak

The spiritual life can only be real
when it is lived in the midst
of the pains and joys
of the here and now.

Making All Things New

The person of hope lives in the moment
with the knowledge and trust
that all of life is in good hands.

Bread for the Journey

Jesus wants us to move
from 'the many things'
to the 'one necessary thing.'

Making All Things New

Chapter 4

Learn God's Ways

*H*ow often we try to make our desires and plans into the will of God. Yet Nouwen reminds us that much of what means so much to us doesn't really matter to God. We who keep expecting God to do things our way need to learn that God's ways are surprisingly different and infinitely more effective than ours.

The things that really matter to God most often take place in private – hidden in plain sight. God chooses the small things we overlook, and Jesus shows us how far God's way of loving can go.

Although God's ways are beyond everything that makes up our life, Nouwen points out that God is "in the center of all of it." God has ways of making the impossible possible and of filling the darkness with light.

It is by being awake
to this God in us
that we can see him
in the world around us.

Clowning in Rome

God is 'beyond'...
all the events and experiences
that make up our life.

Still he is in the center of all of it.

In God's sight,
the things that really matter
seldom take place in public.

Letters to Marc About Jesus

God chooses the small things
which are overlooked
in the big world.

The Road to Daybreak

On the cross
Jesus has shown us
how far God's love goes.

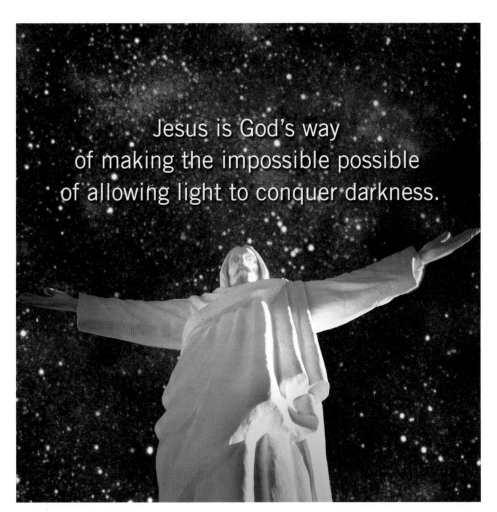

Jesus is God's way
of making the impossible possible
of allowing light to conquer darkness.

The Return of the Prodigal Son

Nurture Your Spiritual Nature

Everyday life encompasses our only chance to become who we really are, Nouwen counsels us. Each day is a God-given opportunity to nurture our spiritual nature. As unique human beings we are each called to realize the potential that is ours alone.

To begin nurturing this hidden or buried nature, we need to "Dare to Be Useless" – we need to stop "doing much" and start "being more."

To appreciate the value of being useless, we need to "Go Deeper" into the reality of who we are – the spiritual nature in which our uniqueness is rooted.

And as we learn to navigate this depth of reality, we gradually begin to "Move to the Center," where we come face to face with our core reality as beloved children of God.

Chapter 5

Dare to Be Useless

We pride ourselves on being useful. But Nouwen often points out that God values our "being" more than our "doing." It is we, not God, who make usefulness a measure of our worth.

Through prayer – by daring to be useless in the divine presence – we show that God is number one in our lives. We set aside time and space in which "nothing" happens.

Time given to this kind of prayer is never wasted. It is we, not God, who are in a hurry. The more we spend time alone with God, the more we sense God's eternal presence with us – at all times and in all places.

Being useless
and silent
in the presence of our God
belongs to the core of all prayer.

Reaching Out

If we really believe...that God...is actively present in our lives... we need to set aside a time and space to give him our undivided attention.

Making All Things New

Contemplative prayer...
is an attitude in which we
recognize God's ultimate
priority by being useless
in his presence.

Clowning in Rome

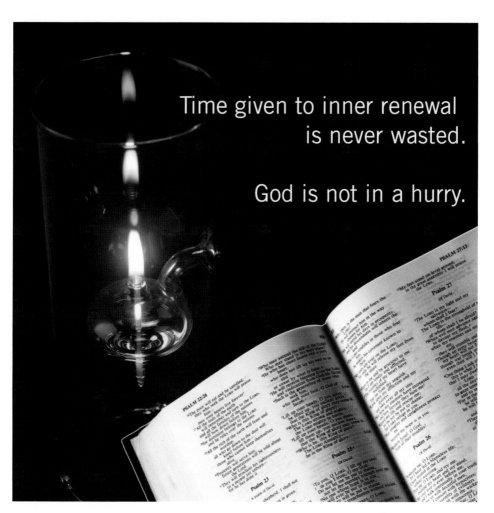

Time given to inner renewal
is never wasted.

God is not in a hurry.

The Road to Daybreak

In solitude
we become aware
that our worth
is not the same
as our usefulness.

Out of Solitude

The more we train ourselves
to spend time with God and him alone
the more we will discover
that God is with us
at all times and
in all places.

Making All Things New

Chapter 6

Go Deeper

To get anyplace in the spiritual life we don't need to go any farther. But we do need to go deeper into our ordinary, everyday experiences. Nouwen advises us that the Spirit of God moves very gently, very persistently, but also very deeply.

The spiritual life is about the heart of existence – where we are most ourselves, most human, most real. It is in the depth of our hearts that we encounter the Spirit. It is in our heart-depth that we touch the hearts of others.

Our inner life is not just for us; it's for all people. The God who dwells within us also makes a home in the inner sacredness of every other human being. As we attune to the deep gentle voice that blesses us, we share the assurance that we are each loved with a depth that is deeper than we can fathom.

The spiritual life
does not remove us from the world
but leads us deeper into it.

Making All Things New

The movement of God's Spirit
is very gentle, very soft…
that movement is also
very persistent, strong and deep.

Life of the Beloved

The spiritual life has to do
with the heart of existence ...

where we are most ourselves,
where we are most human,
where we are most real.

Letters to Marc About Jesus

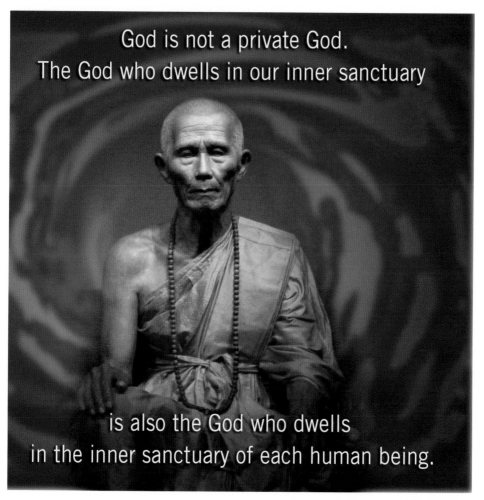

God is not a private God.
The God who dwells in our inner sanctuary

is also the God who dwells
in the inner sanctuary of each human being.

Here and Now

What we live
in the most intimate
places of our beings
is not just for us
but for all people.

Bread for the Journey

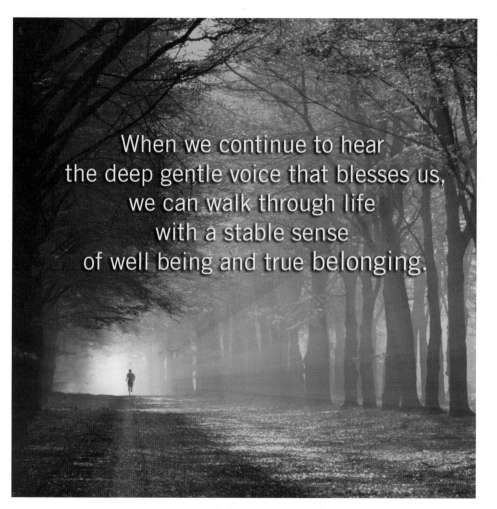

When we continue to hear
the deep gentle voice that blesses us,
we can walk through life
with a stable sense
of well being and true belonging.

Life of the Beloved

Chapter 7

Move to the Center

We who spend so much of our time and energy scurrying around the periphery of our lives need to move to our center. What it means to live spiritually, according to Nouwen, is to live out of the core of our being.

At the center of things is where we meet our Lord in a quiet, unobtrusive way. Living with Jesus at the center makes our life simpler and more focused.

Whenever our worries and fears take us to other places, we need to move our hearts back to the center, where everything falls into place. The spiritual life is a conscious effort to safeguard our inner space, where we can keep our eyes on the Lord.

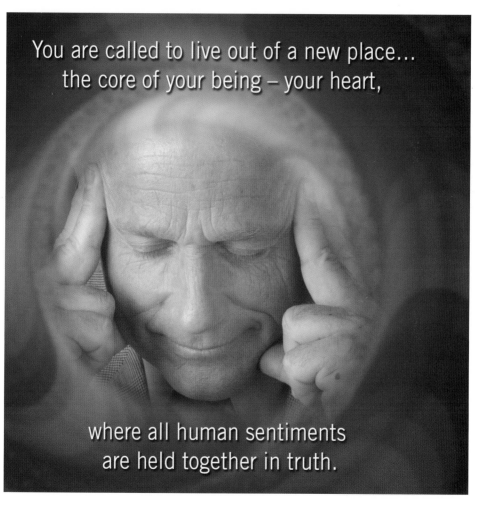

You are called to live out of a new place...
the core of your being – your heart,

where all human sentiments
are held together in truth.

The Inner Voice of Love

The Lord is
at the center of all things...

in such a quiet,
unobtrusive, elusive way.

The Genesee Diary

By allowing the Lord
to be in the center,
life becomes simpler,
more unified,
and more focused.

The Genesee Diary

When we worry,
we have our hearts in the wrong place.

Jesus asks us
to move our hearts to the center,
where all other things
fall into place.

A spiritual life...
requires us to take conscious steps
to safeguard that inner space

where we can keep our eyes
fixed on the beauty of the Lord.

Behold the Beauty of the Lord

Enter into the center of the world
and pray to God from there.

The Genesee Diary

Section III

Share Your Spiritual Life

Once we have finally discovered our spiritual life, Nouwen challenges us to share the treasures we have found. The life of the Spirit is something we're not meant to keep to ourselves.

When we learn to "Live Love," we begin to share one of humankind's best-kept secrets – the joy that compassion can bring into our lives.

The creative Spirit of God always expresses itself in new life. Joy is always connected to birth and rebirth. Every time we share new life we "Present the Presence" to those who may have thought it was absent.

The closer we come to God, the closer we come to our brothers and sisters, and the better equipped we are to truly "Bless the World."

Chapter 8

Live Love

The closer we come to God the closer we come to each other, Nouwen points out repeatedly. Even solitary prayer brings us into deep intimacy with others. Our aloneness with God enables us to meet others in their aloneness.

The more intimate we become with God, the better we are able to treat others as our kin, as our intimate relatives. All hands become God's hands – our own hands that serve others and all the hands that minister to us.

Through the love we share with others we create a home that reveals God's love to our loved ones and to all our guests. Our shared life, dedicated to God, becomes another sign of the divine presence in the world.

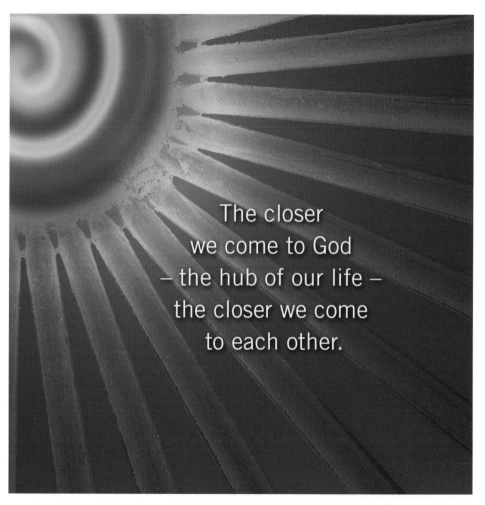

The closer
we come to God
– the hub of our life –
the closer we come
to each other.

The Genesee Diary

When we pray alone…
we enter into a deeper intimacy
with each other.

Clowning in Rome

A growing intimacy with God
creates an always widening space for others.

The Genesee Diary

Community...the place
where we respect, protect,
and reverently greet
one another's aloneness.

Bread for the Journey

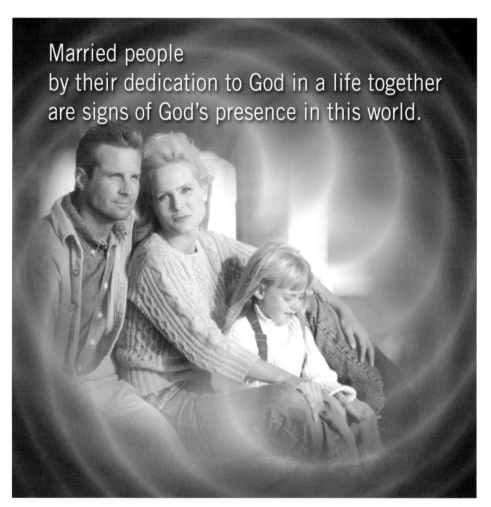

Married people
by their dedication to God in a life together
are signs of God's presence in this world.

Clowning in Rome

Those hands are God's hands...
the hands of my parents,
teachers, friends, healers.

The Return of the Prodigal Son

Chapter 9

Present the Presence

*L*iving a spiritual life is living in the presence of God, advises Nouwen. Even in the midst of our fears and worries we are each called to see God in our world. We are called to make the divine presence visible to others.

Once we have developed eyes for the signs of God's presence, the stars, the mountains, even the smallest wildflower can become entrées into the mysterious godhead. And each person we meet will provide a unique glimpse into the infinite attributes of God.

Living Eucharistically, Nouwen assures us, is already allowing "the other world" to be present in this one. Allowing the presence of God to be present in our lives enables us to be truly present to others.

To live a spiritual life
is to live
in the presence of God.

The Genesee Diary

We are windows
constantly offering each other
new views in the mystery
of God's presence in our lives.

Making All Things New

Often there are flashes
of the presence of God's Spirit
in the midst of our worries.

Making All Things New

And often worries arise even when
we experience the life of the Spirit
in our innermost self.

Making All Things New

Seeing God in the world
and making him visible
to each other is the core
of the contemplative life.

Gracias

The Eucharist...is already the other world present in this one.

The Genesee Diary

Chapter 10

Bless the World

All too often we are too busy to notice that we are being blessed. Nouwen reminds us that we fearful, anxious, insecure human beings all need each other's blessings. Claiming our blessedness inspires us to bless others.

Nouwen challenges us to see ourselves as windows through which we provide a unique view of God's presence among us. Our rich inner life can enrich the lives of all we meet.

Even when we can't cure, we can show how much we care. Even as we walk under a cloudy sky, we can talk about the sun. In the midst of confusion and conflict, we can walk in inner peace. And, like Henri Nouwen, we can each become a blessing to our world.

The problem of modern living
is that we are too busy...
to notice that
we are being blessed.

Life of the Beloved

Claiming your own blessedness
always leads to a deep desire
to bless others.

Life of the Beloved

Often we are not able to cure,
but we are always able to care.

Bread for the Journey

My inner peace
can be a source of peace for all I meet.

The Road to Daybreak

Those who keep speaking about the sun
while walking under a cloudy sky
are messengers of hope,
the true saints of our day.

Here and Now

This Eucharistic life...
keeps faith, hope and love alive in a world
that is constantly
on the brink of self-destruction.

With Burning Hearts

Credits

Acknowledgments

A special thanks to my wife Susan, the soul friend who has shared my spiritual journey for more than four decades. I'm also grateful to our daughter Annette for her typesetting advice, to our son Dan for his design suggestions, as well as to our sons Greg and John for their technical support. And as expressed in the title of one of Henri's books, Gracias to my publisher Greg Pierce, who encouraged my vision for this book.